I WANT TO BE A
ZOOLOGIST

Written by
Valerie Poh

Edited by
Jonathan Reule

Illustration
Carlos Varejão

Storyboard
Keziah Gan

First paperback edition August 2023
ISBN 978-981-17359-1-2

Published by Unibino Pte. Ltd.
31 Rochester Drive Level 3, #03-47 Singapore 138637

www.unibino.com

Zoologists play a vital role in our world when it comes to the relationship between humans and animals. These professionals are experts in animal anatomy, behaviours, classifications and ecology. Their deep understanding of these subjects allows them to unravel the intricate connections between humans and animals, providing valuable insights into our shared ecosystems.

Are you a passionate animal lover who is dedicated to the protection and well-being of our fellow creatures? Do you dream of making a positive impact in the field of zoology? If so, a career as a zoologist might be right for you! This profession is not only fulfilling but also essential in safeguarding the delicate balance of our ecosystems.

But how did a profession such as Zoologist come to be? And why is it so important that we learn how to live harmoniously among the animals we share our planet with? Well, that question is answered by taking a step into the distant past, when we had to understand animal behaviours to help ensure our survival.

In those prehistoric times, before we had great big cities, cars, planes, and other conveniences we take for granted nowadays - we were totally dependent upon the lands. This meant, if we wanted a meal, we had to work for it. But getting food often required us to either follow animals to abundant sources or to use our skills to hunt these creatures, to survive another day.

Although these practices were related to zoology, it wasn't until 1000 BC when we started to observe animals in a more systematic manner. In fact, the ancient Mesopotamians were one of the first civilisations to make detailed records covering a variety of animals.

An example of these records were clay tablets, which described a host of animals from their behaviours to their body shapes and sizes. In many ways, this could be considered some of the first zoological records ever kept.

Of course the Mesopotamians weren't the only civilisation at those times to demonstrate an in-depth knowledge of animals and their inner workings. Did you know that the ancient Egyptians used to embalm and mummify animals to keep them preserved for several thousands of years after they'd died? Well, that's exactly what they did to both humans and animals alike.

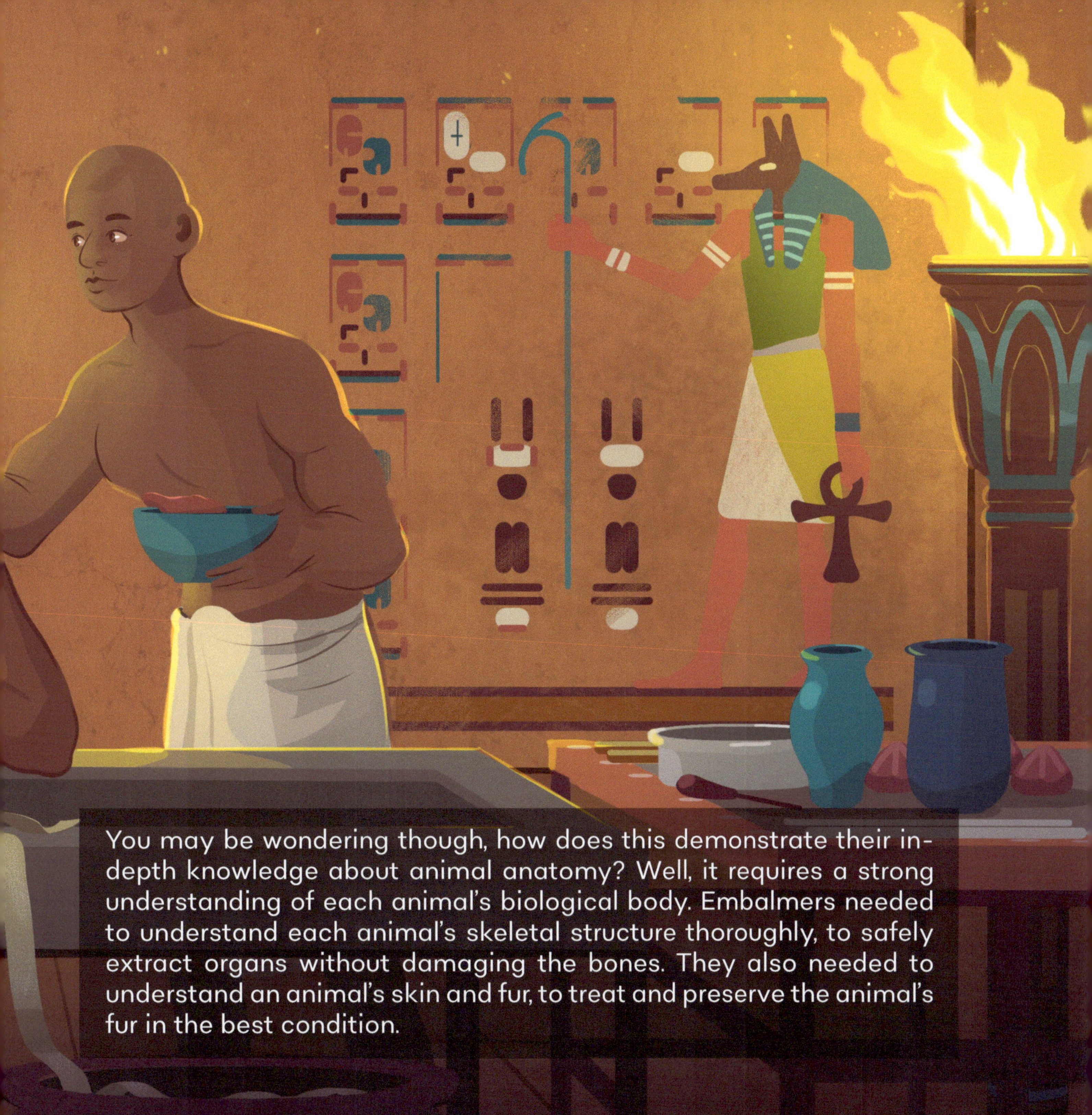

You may be wondering though, how does this demonstrate their in-depth knowledge about animal anatomy? Well, it requires a strong understanding of each animal's biological body. Embalmers needed to understand each animal's skeletal structure thoroughly, to safely extract organs without damaging the bones. They also needed to understand an animal's skin and fur, to treat and preserve the animal's fur in the best condition.

Moving forward to ancient Greece, we encounter a cohort of fervent zoologists, with Aristotle being a prominent figure among them. Born in 384 BC and living until 322 BC, Aristotle is widely recognized as one of the earliest pioneers in the field of zoology. Central to Aristotle's methodology was a profound reliance on observation as the primary means of comprehending the natural world.

Another key contribution that Aristotle made to the study of animals was animal behaviour. He strongly believed that animals behaved in certain ways for a reason. For example, some animal behaviours help them find a mate or find food. Other behaviours help them protect themselves from predators or keep their home safe. Animals also use specific strategies to avoid predators or defend their territories.

One example of Aristotle's emphasis on functional explanations for animal behaviour is his analysis of the behaviour of dolphins. Aristotle observed that dolphins were highly social animals that exhibited complex behaviours such as communication, cooperation, and hunting in groups. He argued that these behaviours were shaped by the function of survival in the aquatic environment.

Aristotle also noted that dolphins used echolocation to locate prey in the water. He argued that the function of this behaviour was to help dolphins identify the location of fish and other food sources in the murky underwater environment. Similarly, he observed that dolphins often cooperated with each other during hunting, working together to herd fish into a confined area where they could be easily caught.

Building upon Aristotle's profound influence on the field of animal studies, the stage is set for the emergence of Charles Darwin's groundbreaking theory of evolution. Prior to Darwin's revolutionary ideas, the prevailing scientific consensus held that animals existed in their present forms, with minimal changes occurring over time.

However, Darwin's groundbreaking work shattered this notion by demonstrating that animals are in a perpetual state of evolution and adaptation.

During his 5-year voyage around the world, Darwin observed variations in similarities and differences between species in different regions. This suggested to him that animals were adapted to their environments in specific ways.

One example from Charles Darwin's book 'On the Origin of Species' is his discussion of the variation in beak size among Galapagos finches. Darwin observed that the finches had evolved different beak shapes and sizes depending on the types of food available on each island of the Galapagos archipelago.

We can see that studying animals has been a fundamental part of human culture since the earliest of times. In the beginning, we seek to understand animals so that we can find food to survive. This interest in the lives of animals carries on into modern times, as we seek to keep understanding the natural world and our relationship with it, while also wanting to increase conservation efforts for animals and their habitats.

Thankfully the many advancements in technology and transportation over the past few decades have greatly benefitted the field of zoology. Faster and more efficient transportation, such as ships and aeroplanes, now allow zoologists to explore and discover new species in remote and previously inaccessible areas of the world. For example, the invention of the submarine and scuba diving equipment has allowed researchers to study marine life in greater detail.

Technological advances have also made fieldwork more efficient and effective. For example, GPS technology has made it easier to track the movements of animals in the wild, while remote sensing technologies like drones and satellite imagery can be used to study animal behaviour and habitat from afar.

Advances in computing and data storage have also enabled zoologists to collect and analyze vast amounts of data about animals and their behaviour. This has led to a greater understanding of how animals interact with their environment, and how changes in the environment can impact their behaviour and survival.

So if you are deeply fascinated by animals and want a career that helps you to understand them better, being a zoologist would help you study them in almost any way you want! But first; a love for animals is not enough to get you into this career. Here are some steps you need to take to become a zoologist.

To become a zoologist, you typically need to obtain a bachelor's degree in biology, zoology, or a related field. During your studies, you will take courses in subjects such as genetics, animal behaviour, ecology, and evolution. You may then choose to specialize in a particular area of zoology, such as marine biology, ornithology (the study of birds), mammalogy (the study of mammals), or herpetology (the study of reptiles and amphibians, etc.).

Marine Biology
ORNITHOLOGY
HERPETOLOGY

While obtaining a bachelor's or graduate degree in zoology or a related field is the most common path to becoming a zoologist, there are also other ways to enter the field. You could gain experience through internships or volunteer work.

Many zoos, wildlife centres, and research organizations offer internships or volunteer positions to students or individuals interested in pursuing a career in zoology. This can provide valuable hands-on experience working with animals and conducting research.

As a zoologist, there are many different avenues for you depending on your interests and career goals. Many zoologists work in academic or research settings, conducting experiments and studies to better understand the behaviour, ecology, physiology, and evolution of animals. This may involve working in a laboratory, conducting fieldwork, or analyzing data.

Zoologists can work for government agencies, non-profit organizations, or private companies focused on conserving and protecting wildlife and their habitats. They work together to create and implement conservation plans, conduct environmental assessments, or educate the public about conservation issues.

RVATION DAY

Some zoologists may choose to become veterinarians, working to diagnose and treat diseases and injuries in animals. Some zoologists also work in zoos and aquariums, caring for and studying captive animals. This may involve designing and implementing enrichment programs, conducting research, or educating the public about the animals on display.

Zoologists can also work for government agencies or private companies to manage and regulate wildlife populations, including conducting surveys, setting hunting and fishing quotas, and developing policies and regulations. Some zoologists may also choose to work in science communication, sharing their knowledge and research with the public through writing, broadcasting, or other media.

These are just a few examples of the different avenues available for zoologists. The field of zoology is broad and diverse, and there are many opportunities for individuals with different backgrounds and interests to make a difference in the lives of animals.

Overall, the role of a zoologist is to increase our understanding of animals and their interactions with their environment, and to use this knowledge to improve our management and conservation efforts for these important organisms. Is this a career that sparks an interest for you? Time to listen to your love for animals and follow your passion!

Shubhi Saxena
Founder, Unibino

My Inspiration

As a parent in this ever-changing world, it can sometimes feel overwhelming when it comes to our children's futures. New technologies seem to be arising almost every day, and with so many innovations, it creates unique professions which many of us wouldn't have dreamed to be necessary only a few years ago. Which to me is a good thing. Because with so much variety, my children can have the opportunity to pick a career that will fit their personalities and build upon their strengths. As you may imagine, this desire within me to provide my children with the resources they needed to thrive, led me to search out books that would be easy enough for them to understand while teaching them about various professions.

Only, I found that these books were few and far between. Even if I could find a book about a certain profession geared towards young readers, I found them sparse inside and limited to only certain careers that may not fit my children's abilities. This is when I came up with the idea to write my own children's books, teaching them about all the various careers in the modern world. After months of researching different professions and learning more than I ever expected, I quickly realised this was going to be a bigger project than I first anticipated. I dove into the histories of these professions, discovering links to the past, and why these professions were now so important.

Ultimately my goal was to offer my children options, to show them that there is no one set path for everyone. But in this, I stumbled upon something bigger. I wanted to share this with future generations. To share with all children and parents about these careers, to help spark curiosity, and to instil a passion for the future. Everyone has special talents and abilities, and I hope that this series will be able to offer clarity and inspiration to children around the world. Because at the end of the day, it's never too early to start dreaming and never too late to take action. With this, I hope you enjoy this series and that your young ones become the best versions of themselves as they can achieve.